NOTE.—Copies will be forwarded on the receipt of postage stamps, by the Author, SAMUEL CATTON, No. 1, Ebenezer Place, Plaistow Park, E.

A Short Sketch of a Long Life

OF

SAMUEL CATTON,

ONCE A SUFFOLK PLOUGH-BOY.

PRICE THREEPENCE.

LONDON:

ARPTHORPE, Bishopsgate Street. CAUDWELL, 335, Strand, W.C.

IPSWICH:

REES AND GRIPPER, Cornhill.

1863.

A SHORT SKETCH

OF

A LONG LIFE

OF

SAMUEL CATTON,

ONCE A SUFFOLK PLOUGH-BOY,

SHOWING WHAT PRAYER AND PERSEVERANCE MAY DO.

PRICE THREEPENCE.

LONDON:
ARPTHORPE, Bishopsgate St. CAUDWELL, 335, Strand, W.C.
IPSWICH:
REES AND GRIPPER, Cornhill.

G. HARMER, PRINTER, WEST HAM.

MEMOIR OF S. CATTON.

CHAPTER I.

THE object of this Memoir is (the author has desired) that it might be the means of stimulating other young people to persevere so as to make themselves useful, as he has endeavoured to do in his day and generation. He does not write this to exalt the creature, but wishes to ascribe it all to a kind Providence in lengthening his life till the present period, as he is now in the 75th year of his age, and has nothing to depend upon but Jesus Christ our Lord and Saviour. We find our friend SAMUEL CATTON was born in the year 1788, in a small village called Eyke, near Woodbridge, in Suffolk, of poor parents, and was the youngest of eight children. He was particularly attached to his mother, as she was of a pious inclination. We find him going out to service when he was only about ten or twelve years of age, where he was employed in looking after cattle in that neighbourhood, which happened in the year 1800. We find he gives an account last year of Margaret Catchpole, which letter may be seen in the book of her life, *p.* 379.

In 1801-2-3 we find him engaged at a timber carter's in the village where he was born; and in 1804 he went to live at a place called Tunstall, where he learnt to hold the plough, of which employment he was particularly fond. At this place he was called "Little Sam," as there was another, older than him, who they called "Big Sam." In 1805 he was engaged in a village named Bramfield, about sixteen miles from his residence, where he was very uncomfortable, and cruelly treated, as his master and mistress were both drunkards, and the only son was very often deranged. His master offered to engage him the second year, but he refused. In 1806 he returned home to his parents, and remained at home a week, the only week that he was out of a situation for fifteen years, so you will say he did not lead an idle life. In 1806-7 he obtained a place at Eyke, where he lived two years. The next place we find him engaged at was Woodbridge, where he remained till the year 1810. Here he was wrought upon by the kind Providence of God, and often tried to pray. Here he paid a little boy 6d. per week to teach him to read and write. After stopping at this place upwards of two years he found himself exposed to many temptations, and was anxious to get away from his gay companions. A gentleman coming from London engaged him, where he stopped till 1811, and in July he took to himself a wife, and became employed at some Chemical works at Stratford, near London, for eight or nine years, under the care of his wife's uncle, and, as he was expert in the Chemical Works he had very good wages;

but his health giving way at the latter place he was advised to quit this employment, as he had every symptoms of consumption.

CHAPTER II.

The author cannot proceed with this narrative without referring to several things that transpired in the neighbourhood of Eyke, Woodbridge, Wickham Market, and other places adjoining, in Suffolk. A person by the name of Thomson, of Culphoe Hall, was engaged to preach in different parts of the neighbourhood, and was the means of establishing upwards of thirty places of worship amongst the Dissenters. The author has known him to travel miles in the week to preach, and also on Sundays. He was made an instrument in the hands of a kind Providence in establishing chapels at Grundisburgh, Wickham Market, Tunstall, and Bromeswell. At the latter place the author of this narrative and another boy went to hear him preach, being the first Dissenting minister he had ever heard; and he was grieved whilst there to hear some of the rude rabble make scoffing remarks, and the preacher made a stop, and told them that he did not come there to take away their money, but to tell them for their good, which made a great impression upon the author of this narrative. Upon our returning home, and having some way to walk, we were rather behind time for our suppers, and on going in our master enquired where we had been, and I, with an audible voice, before them all, said, "To the meeting, sir," and my old master ordered us both out from supper, and said that we might go back where we had been, as we should have no supper there. (The above preacher was distributing hymn books.) I and the other boy went quietly to bed, sorry that we had been dealt with so unkindly by our master, as we had done all our work before going to meeting.

This dear old man as he travelled from place to place suffered great persecution, as the neighbourhood of Wickham Market and other places were infested by smugglers and other desperate characters. One Sunday the rabble got a waggon full of bread for distribution, and the man that distributed it was a sort of Merry Andrew with his wig 'hind part before; and oft times they went into the preaching place, throwing in rotten eggs and stinking sprats. At last some of the ringleaders were taken up before the Woodbridge Magistrates, and, after hearing both sides of the question, they were dismissed. The bells were rang at Woodbridge and Wickham Market, because they had beaten the Dissenters; but the Dissenters afterwards moved for a fresh trial at the Queen's Bench, where they had justice done them; some were fined, and others were severely reprimanded. This partly put a stop to the persecution against the Dissenters, and many of the parties came to an untimely end. This dear old man also suffered much through some of his family. Two of his sons were engaged in malting, at Woodbridge. They, not following the integrity of their father, ran the duty, were found out, and heavily fined, which ruined the poor old father, and he had to make an appeal to the religious public in 1812.

CHAPTER III.

One of these smugglers, who was called "Little Dick," was the ringleader of a desperate gang near Wickham Market. The author has seen above a dozen carts going down from his house to Hollesley Bay, and other parts of the seaside, when there was a smuggling cutter come in laden with gin, tobacco, and other things which have a heavy duty in this country, and there used to be desperate fights between these smugglers and the revenue officers, and they used to cut and hack each other about more like demons than human beings. This "Little Dick" had been drinking with one of the revenue officers at the Sun Inn, Woodbridge, and both going home the worse for liquor, he told the revenue officer that he would show him how the smugglers run away from them, and he stuck his spurs into his "Brown Betty," and when he got as far as Petistree Tuns, which was within a mile of his own house, she threw him off, and his head came in contact with a milestone, which brought on concussion of the brain; he never spoke afterwards. Another circumstance—a person came to live in the neighbourhood of Woodbridge, with great wealth, at the latter end of the eighteenth century. He bought a great many farms, and cut and hacked them about (to the great annoyance of the farmers) to raise game, but his career was not very long, for in September, 1808, being the first day of the shooting season, he was out with a party, and a gentleman in the neighbourhood was shooting on another manor, when he rode up and ordered him off; he turned his pony round, and being greatly excited, fell off, and died on the spot in a fit of apoplexy. One more circumstance before I go on with my narrative. Mr. W. Kell died in the eighty-third year of his age, in the Seckford Almshouses, Woodbridge, on the 15th of February, 18—, whose long life in that place abounded in incidents both curious and extraordinary—having been at times the subject of grave consideration, and at others of the greatest mirth. Among the most remarkable events of William Kell's life are the following :—he married and survived no less than five wives, four of whom had issue. The number of his children amounted to thirty. He was born at Woodbridge, and resided in that town the whole of his life. He was apprenticed to a hairdresser, and followed, at subsequent times, the following employments: shoemaker, razor-grinder, publican, coach and harness maker, sign, house, and ornamental painter, engraver, and grave stone cutter. He was principal violin player at all the balls and country dances, and gave lessons on the violin, and taught dancing. He was also principal chorister in the church; and, by way of variety, he studied, and was celebrated for his exhibition of the famous Punch and Judy, as also the mystic art of conjuration. He serenaded the town for more than fifty years as leader of the Christmas Waits. He served his country's cause as Band-Major in the Woodbridge Loyal Volunteers, trumpeter in the Yeomanry Cavalry, drummer in the Sea Fencibles, and horn player in the band of the Local Militia, and his last public function was that of Town Crier, for which office he was peculiarly adapted, as he had a good pronunciation and a fine clear voice. He retained this office till his admission (six years since) into the Seckford Almshouses. He cheered with his vocal powers the brethren of the Masonic and Druidic Lodges, of which he was a member; and, say what more we can or may, all must admit that he was, in the true acceptation of the word, an "Odd Fellow." (Taken from the *Ipswich Express* a few years ago.)

CHAPTER IV.

In resuming his narrative the author has been extraordinarily delivered from many accidents, which are as follow : He once narrowly escaped death by strangulation, and once narrowly escaped, when very young, by the overturning of a cart, he being inside at the time; but though much bruised, yet, after a few weeks, he recovered. Another time himself and a young man were bathing at the New Quay, Woodbridge, and after the author came out the other young man was drawn into a strong current of the river, and by turning round to face the current he sank like a stone. He (the author) plunged in after him, providentially saving him, though they were both struggling in the water. I will relate one more, which happened a few years ago. Walking along in Lombard Street, some workmen were lowering a lot of bricks from a scaffolding, and a lump of old ones, about five cwt., were being lowered into a cart, and coming too heavy on the horse's back rolled off the cart, within a yard of the author, narrowly escaping being crushed to death.

CHAPTER V.

He was a regular attender at the "particular" Baptists, at the Old Ford, Dr. Newman being minister there. After attending there about two years he applied for membership, and he and nine females were publicly admitted by immersion, before a large assembly there gathered. He was a regular attendant for about eight years, but he became very uneasy about the doctrine of predestination, and, after duly considering, he felt it to be his duty to withdraw from them. After much prayer and exercise of mind he sent in his resignation as a member, though he was particularly attached to the minister and the congregation. Falling in with some popular works of the Religious Society of Friends, such as George Fox, Thomas Chalkley's Journal, and Sewell's History of that Society, he read them with care and prayer, and saw it his duty to join them, after attending their religious meetings for two years.

After being connected with this religious society above forty years, he now feels it his duty to bear a testimony to their principles, which are founded on Christ, the only hope of Salvation. Our last yearly meetings' epistle (1862) will show forth its fundamental doctrines, founded on Him alone. Although this religious society has had many struggles within the last fifty years, and some alterations in Church discipline during the last two or three years, yet he believes that the alteration will tend to the benefit of this religious society and the prosperity of Christ. About two or three years back many weighty friends were appointed by our yearly meeting, to re-consider and make some improvements in Church discipline, which are brought forth in the fourth edition of extracts from the Minutes and Epistles of the Yearly Meeting of the Religious Society of Friends.

Chapter VI.

As mentioned in a former page, my health rapidly gave way at the Chemical Works. In the year 1820 I took a general shop at Plaistow, and continued for thirty-six years; after struggling there for the above period, with a large family, I gave it up in 1856, and my labours with the young for the last forty years have been very great; and now, at the decline of my life, I have much to look back and be thankful for to the Almighty, and can say, "hitherto the Lord hath helped me." The thousands and tens of thousands of children that I have stood before with the Magic Lantern, Chemical Lectures, and other amusements. I feel thankful that I have never scarcely omitted to recommend the Bible, and the building their hopes on the Lord Jesus Christ, as the only sure foundation for us to be saved.

Chapter VII.

Being fond of children from my youth, I have often felt an anxious desire for the rising generation in the neighbourhood in which I was born; and as much good had been done in and about the neighbourhood where I lived (Plaistow), in the Sunday Schools, I became very anxious to make some effort in trying to establish

Sunday Schools at Eyke and Rendlesham, and, after
duly considering it, I believed it was my duty to write
to the clergyman of the village (about forty years ago),
who had officiated there about thirty years, and I
pleaded with him to take up the subject for the poor
children, but he, growing an old man, and one of the
old school, thought that the farmers and the gentry
round about would not fall in with my proposition.
Several months after I went down to my native village,
and spoke to some of the Dissenting friends, one
young man in particular, named Rouse, who was a
popular preacher at that time in that locality, and one
of his deacons, named Clarke, they soon fell in with
my proposition; they formed a Sunday School in an
old barn, and was very successful in establishing a
Sunday School at Rendlesham, at which place young
Rouse preached several years. About twelve months
after I went down I paid another visit, and found nearly
two hundred children present on the Lord's Day in the
old barn. It went on in a prosperous way for a few
years. At last the old clergyman, whom I wrote to,
went the way of all flesh, and another clergyman, named
Groom, was appointed in his stead; and, as the school
continued prosperous, the two clergymen at Eyke and
Rendlesham became jealous of the old barn, and they
told the teachers that they were draining all the children away from the two churches, and they proposed
to the superintendent of the barn to form two schools,
one at Eyke and one at Rendlesham, in their two
churches, and proposed to take the school materials off

their hands. The above friends wrote to me about it, and I wrote back again, telling them to be sure and fall in with it, for it was just what I wanted, as it looked rather a sectarian movement in the old barn, and two schools were soon established at the churches, and have continued from that time to the present, and I believe it has been the means of doing a great deal of good. (In the Sunday School Correspondence see the letter which I wrote to the clergyman at Eyke, *p.* 13.) About sixteen or seventeen years ago, Lady Rendlesham, seeing the children attend the aforesaid schools on Sunday, enquired where they had their education on the week day, and it was answered that there were no public schools in the neighbourhood, and this dear lady had a large school built at Rendlesham for boys and girls, and they have continued it in a prosperous condition from that time to the present. Many of the inhabitants said that I ought to have laid the first brick of that school, as it was a plant that sprung out of the old barn. And another circumstance gave me great satisfaction: three or four years ago a new clergyman was appointed at Eyke, and through his efforts, and the kind friends round about him, an Infant School was established at Eyke, about a mile from the Girls' and Boys' School. Last September I paid another visit. There I found this interesting Infant School, and also a Sunday School for the parish of Eyke. The time I was there I walked with about a hundred children from this school to the church on the Lord's Day, and some of the inhabitants, while I was walking with them, called out, "Mr. Catton, you are still amongst the young." I was much pleased with the mistress, as I believed she was a pious woman, and had the welfare of the children at heart. I was also pleased to see the good conduct of the children while the religious service was going on in the church. And the same evening I attended a cottage meeting, crammed to suffocation, and at the conclusion of the service I addressed those that were present, and said that I had been removed from that locality about fifty-five years, and, though I was not known to many of them, yet I had always a lively interest for that village (Eyke), and perhaps it would be my last visit amongst them. I left them with a lively feeling, wishing that the Lord would prosper them when I should be under the clods of the valley. At the conclusion of the meeting I distributed about two hundred of Mr. Curwen's Hymn Books, British Workmen, and Bands of Hope. After spending about four days with them I took my leave, expecting never to see them again. I turned back to Woodbridge, spent about four days there, and then went to Ipswich. I visited many friends there, and took the chair at a large temperance meeting, in the Temperance Hall, and returned home very satisfied with, perhaps, my last visit into Suffolk.

CHAPTER VIII.

About fifty years ago, I and about a dozen friends were picked out to form a Bible Society, at West Ham. We had formed districts in the parish, and I and another was appointed to district number one, which reached from Bow Bridge to Stratford Turnpike. Many of us were successful in collecting money for Bibles and free subscriptions. The Secretary, Henry Cockfield, Esq., wrote to Archdeacon Jones (who was then Vicar of West Ham), asking him to become President of the Bible Society, but he sent an abrupt letter to the Secretary, and said that he should not join us because we did not distribute the Prayer Book at the same time, which we could not consistently fall in with. After due consideration we appointed Samuel Gurney, Esq., of Ham House, President, which office he filled till the day of his death, with much lively interest for the Bible, and for schools in the parish of West Ham. After it had been established a few years, we agreed to establish a Ladies' Society in lieu of the gentlemen, which has been carried on with a lively interest from the commencement; and I have had the pleasure of distributing the monthly extracts, which have been supplied by a lady in the neighbourhood, and which give me great satisfaction. About twenty-six years back, Henry Althans was appointed from the Borough Road School to pay us a visit in the parish of West Ham, to canvass the parish, and he made it appear before us that there were hundreds of boys who had no opportunity to get a cheap education, and we found Mr. Witty in a small school at Stratford Marsh, with the small salary of 16s. per week. After a short time the British School, in Little North Street, Stratford, was built, and he officiated as master there for some years, with much success, and after him Mr. Combs, till he removed to India; and at the present time there are two interesting masters, Messrs. Brewer and Smith, and about one hundred and seventy boys on the books. I have been on the committee since the commencement, and have felt a lively interest in its welfare. I can bear testimony to the much good *that* school has done since it has been established ; and at the decease of Samuel Gurney, Esq., he endowed the Boys' School at £100 per year, and the Girls' School, in Bridge Street, at £50 per year.

About three years back I wrote eight letters to the Editor of the *Stratford Times*, under the head of the " Old Inhabitant," viz., what the parish of West Ham was fifty years back, and what it was then. We passed through the several districts, beginning at Bow Bridge, and finishing the eighth at the Victoria Docks. These letters were read with great interest, the reader often wondering who the " Old Inhabitant " was ; and it often made the author smile to hear the different remarks, particularly the third letter, which gives an account of the martyrdom at Stratford, viz., the burning of thirteen martyrs at Stratford. Now, after going through the parish, he concluded about the increase of churches, chapels, and schools, in the aforesaid parish, viz., fifty years ago there was but one church, four chapels, and three schools. Then (1860) there were six churches, twenty-four chapels, and thirty schools, which last were attended by upwards of four thousand one hundred and fifty children ; and still, for the last three years, there has been several other churches, chapels, and schools built. For the last three years many improvements have taken place in the parish of West Ham, for instance, the under drainage, under the inspection of the Board of Health, and the High Level Sewer through our parish (West Ham), reaching from Victoria Park to Barking Creek. London has now reached down (within the last fifty-three years) from Mile End to Stratford, and from Limehouse to the Abbey Arms, at Plaistow, so our parish is now called "London over the Borders." The health of the parish of West Ham will be much benefitted by the underground drainage, and London will be materially improved by the High Level Sewer which carries the filth as far out as Barking Creek. The High Level Sewer reaches above five miles—from Victoria Park to Barking Creek, which is composed of three large arches, about nine feet high, and there are six bridges crossing the sewer, viz., one at Old Ford, one at Stratford, three at Plaistow, and one at East Ham ; and the Tilbury and Southend Railway runs under the sewer near the Plaistow Station. The line of the Great Eastern Railway runs over the sewer, and the North Woolwich runs under it. The height of the sewer is from twenty to thirty feet above the surface at some places.

Chapter IX.

About twenty-six years ago I was appointed by the late Samuel Gurney, Esq., of Ham House, to be superintendent of the allotments of land in Plaistow. I filled that office eight or nine years, but he extended them to other parts of the parish, and I had to give up my office, one person being appointed to superintend the whole. I can bear testimony to the good effect they have had on the working classes generally; but even in this we had opposition from the farmers. I have travelled hundreds of miles and collected information, and advocated its claims for the Labourer's Friend Society, and they presented me with a volume for the valuable information that I had given them, in different letters, which came into print at that time.

And about the same time I was invited by a friend by the name of Richard Barrett to attend a meeting in Bishopsgate Street, to meet a gentleman from Glasgow, by the name of Dr. Colosson. There were about sixteen of us took tea together at a friend's by the name of Hargraves. We formed a society, the "Temperance, or Moderation Society," which was to discontinue the use of ardent spirits, such as rum, gin, brandy, and whisky, but wine, beer, or cider, might be taken in moderation. There were then present—Thomas Shellitoe, Hannah Kellum, Richard Barrett, John Capper, and S. Catton, and many others, whose names I have forgotten. We all set to work in earnest in the Moderation Movement, and I remained a member for about eight or nine years, and we had two or three meetings in Exeter Hall, with the Bishop of London in the chair. In this Moderation Society we had bishops and clergymen join us by wholesale. Still, after struggling with this for some time, we found that drunkenness still went on, and that people got the worse for liquor by beer, wine, and cider. At length seven men at Preston started a society, called the Total Abstinence Society, and a lecturer, named Livesay, came up to London, and several others, to lecture to do away with all intoxicating drinks. The Total Abstinence principle spread very rapidly in London and different parts of the country, and it was soon like Aaron's rod, swallowed up the old Moderation Society, though it was the stepping-stone to Total Abstinence, and in 1828 this question was begun at Stratford, by a few praying Christians, and they began to advocate its claims at Plaistow, Bow, Stratford, Leytonstone, and many other places. Several of its friends tried to get me to sign the total abstinence pledge, but, I then being fond of my home brewed beer, and thought that they were going to an extreme, I refused for some time, but after duly considering it, with an earnest prayer to be directed right, I signed it for three months. After I had signed the pledge for three months it spread rapidly in Plaistow and its neighbourhood that Mr. Catton had become a total abstainer. 'Tis true I missed my home brewed beer, and I subjected myself to many remarks, that I should soon be in my grave, and they said that I was rapidly falling away in flesh. When the three months were up there was a large meeting in Plaistow National School, and many said that I was about taking my name off the pledge-book, as it would not suit me, but I kept my mind quiet, and prayed to be directed in the right way. When I signed the total abstinence pledge I promised my hearers that at the expiration of the three months' trial I would come forward and let them know how it suited me, and at the three months' end I went forward, amid a crowded audience, and told them truly that I did miss my home brewed beer at first, but as I had set my hand to the plough, I was determined not to look back, and saw it my duty to go on with it, trusting for help from above. We soon had the publicans and the rude rabble to disturb us in our meetings at Plaistow and elsewhere. At the expiration of the first year we had the pledges of fourteen reclaimed drunkards; at the end of the second we had thirty-eight, besides many moderationists; and at the end of the third year we had eighty-four, amongst whom were several notorious drunken females, and as our meetings were oftentimes very boisterous from the rude rabble, and some of the teetotallers could no tkeep their tempers. Archdeacon Jones turned us out of the National School at West Ham, and also at Plaistow.

A few months after we had been turned out of the National School, Samuel Catton consulted some of his friends at Plaistow and Stratford about building a hall at Plaistow, and mentioned this to some of his friends that he intended to have such a place built. He told them that he would collect money for the above purpose from one penny and upwards, and a little girl, about six years of age, gave him the first penny towards it, and a little girl, in the same family, asked her mother if she might give Mr. Catton a shilling out of her box towards building the Temperance Hall. In a few months he had collected about £80 for the aforesaid hall, and after a suitable site was found, it was built, in the year 1840. The whole money that Samuel Catton collected was £160, the rest was collected by some of his friends in the neighbourhood, and it cost about £200. It was opened in August, 1840, with tea, and three public meetings, three days in succession, on the first of which Samuel Catton was presented with a handsome silver medal, bearing the following inscription : " 19th August, 1840. Presented by the Stratford Committee to Samuel Catton, for his unwearied exertions in the temperance cause." Meetings have been held ever since on a Thursday night, and much good has resultd, such as reclaiming many a poor drunkard. At the commencement of the temperance movement Plaistow was held as a branch of the Total Abstinence Society at Stratford, and it went on prosperous for about four or five years, and some of our religious friends removed from us, and we had to change committees several times. Some of the teetotallers of Stratford (about eighteen years ago) wanted to have fiddling and dancing in the aforesaid hall on the day called Christmas, and Samuel Catton and some of his friends had to make a stand against that proposition, though with much opposition, and he and his friends concluded to separate from the aforesaid Society, and above a hundred was for us to become a society by ourselves, called the Plaistow Total Abstinence Society. We began our meetings by reading the scriptures, believing that if ever the Total Abstinence Society flourishes it must flourish under Christian principle.

Chapter X.

For the last twenty-two years that hall has been made great use of, for lectures for the Peace Society, Anti-Slavery Society, and Sunday School. About two years back the Methodists applied to Samuel Catton to be allowed to preach in the hall, which was carried on on a Sunday, we hope with some success, and last Christmas they withdrew the preachers suddenly, though no reason was assigned; but Samuel Catton and two or three of the Missionaries consulted together, and we considered that from forty to fifty persons used to assemble there on a Sunday evening, and we concluded to have religious service there, to be continued on the broad scale of Christianity, connected with no religious society; we take Christ to be the head of our Church. There is reading the Scriptures, as usual, and singing and prayer, and we do not throw any objection to any one, either male or female, for all are one in Christ. The service commences at half-past six p.m., and ends at eight, and sometimes there are three or four have a little to say to encourage each other, and our meetings thus far have been held with great solemnity, and much comfort. We believe that Christ came into the world to die for all. We recommend our members to study the Holy Scriptures, particularly the New Testament. It hath God for its author, Salvation for its end, and Truth, without mixture of error; and we advise our members to abstain from all intoxicating drinks, particularly the preachers, for that has been a great barrier to the Church of Christ in other denominations. **Nearly** two years ago some of our friends undertook to get up a Free School in the Hall, and there is from 80 to 100 children attend regularly. Mrs. Burnes, one of our Missionaries wives, the Missionary of Plaistow, and afterwards his wife carried it on with much success but her health not continuing, a suitable mistress was found in Miss Stubbs. These poor children are educated, and were sometimes fed and clothed during the last two winters by our much esteemed friend, Miss Crossland, and other ladies, whom we style the Dorcas of Plaistow. She and other ladies take a lively interest in it, and through her exertions the mistress is allowed £30 a year, and the poor children seem to be much improved. The last two months she collected money to make some alteration in the hall for a class-room and accommodation for the children. The hall has been repaired and is now neat and comfortable, which cost about £20, that sum Miss Crossland collected from some of our wealthy friends.

The PLAISTOW SCHOOL CHILDREN'S DRINKING FOUNTAIN, which SAMUEL CATTON undertook to collect money for, answers very well, the cost of which was £63. The 600 children belonging to the three schools found it a great accommodation last summer, and the washing troughs for children, horses' drinking troughs, and the place for dogs, have been made much use of since the fountain was opened in 1861; but much annoyance has been experienced by the rude children in the neighbourhood destroying the mugs, but we hope it has partly subsided. The names of the 200 subscribers whose contributions range from £7 to 1d. may be seen in the Plaistow Temperance Hall.

SAMUEL CATTON feels greatly obliged to those ladies and gentlemen who have assisted him with their subscriptions, and also for the kindness which has been shown him for so long a period.

In Conclusion, we just remark that he filled the office of door-keeper at the Friends' Meeting at Plaistow for 12 years, and made himself useful at Plaistow and elsewhere for a period of 43 years, and he feels very grateful to his wealthy friends that they have not forgotten him in his decline of years, and can say—"Hitherto the Lord has helped me."

"West Ham Local Board of Health, 17th July, 1862.

"SIR,—I am directed by the Local Board of Health to inform you that they have agreed to take the Drinking Fountains mentioned in your letter of the 29th ult. from the 24th June last.

"I am, Sir, yours respectfully,

"J. KNOTT,

"Clerk *pro tem.*

"Samuel Catton, Plaistow.

"N.B. The fountains are placed under Samuel Catton's care by the Board of Health, as long as he lives."

The following is extracted from the *Stratford Times* of March 21st, 1863 :—

"WALTHAMSTOW BRITISH DAY SCHOOLS.—On the marriage-day of the Prince of Wales and the Princess Alexandra, Mrs. H. F. BARCLAY, with her usual liberality and great kindness, provided a treat to the above schools, which consisted in a good supply of buns, ginger-beer, oranges, &c. After the youngsters had done full justice to the good things set before them, ' Father Catton' entertained the young folks by an exhibition with his phantasmagoria lantern. No sooner were the young folks seated than the dear old man struck up one of his favourite tunes, which was well known, and taken up heartily by all present. Every countenance was lit up with smiles and twinkling eyes on seeing the old patriarch pacing to and fro, stick in hand, with all the fervour of a young enthusiast. Who could not help being happy where 'Father Catton' was? His old blood seemed to circulate with fresh vigour. He loves the young—they know it, and their little hearts in return overflow with love to him. His metallic voice, attitude, either standing or walking, and humorous sayings, tended most unmistakeably to make a great impression upon all present. The lecture was interspersed with the dear old man's warbling and sayings—sayings which were fraught with wisdom and humour, and would bear comparison with those of that philosophic sage Benjamin Franklin. Temperance, cleanliness, truthfulness, kindness to animals (not forgetting our fellow-men), obedience to parents, and taking the Bible for our rule and guide, found a prominent place in his advice to the young folks. At the close of the lecture Mr. Blamires, C.M., offered a few appropriate remarks, at the close of which three cheers were given for Mrs. H. F. Barclay, and the same number were repeated for the Master and Mistress, and 'Father Catton.' If loud and continued cheering be a true token of loyalty and patriotism, the concluding cheers given for the Prince of Wales and Princess Alexandra and our beloved Queen, the company present stood A 1 for love of country and the Royal family."

PLAISTOW
Band of Hope, or Juvenile Abstainers.

S. CATTON	...	...	...	...	PRESIDENT.
Mr. DAVIS	...	...	...	...	SUPERINTENDENT.
E. PARKER	...	...	...	...	SECRETARY.

TO THE SECRETARY,

SIR,—I wish to become a Member of the above Society, having obtained the consent of my parents, and I promise to abstain from all intoxicating liquors as a beverage, and from tobacco, and by advice and example to seek to prevent their use by others.

Plainly
Written.
{ Name_____

Address_____

Age_____

*** This Paper when filled up is to be returned to S. CATTON, President, at the next meeting of the Society, and at the end of one month the applicant will be entitled to a Member's Certificate, and all the privileges of the Society.

Swifty our moments pass away,
　And soon they all will disappear;
May we endeavour while 'tis day,
　To teach the young their God to fear.

Soon will the final hour arrive
　When all our toil and care will cease;
O may we all with ardour strive,
　To guide the young in paths of peace.

Dear Saviour, own our care and bless
　Each weak attempt to spread thy name;
Vain will each effort prove useless
　Thy blessing rest upon the same.

But if our labour thou approve,
　Success upon it will attend;
And we, in this employ of love,
　Our happiest hours on earth shall spend.

INDEX.

www.ingramcontent.com/pod-product-compliance
Lightning Source LLC
Chambersburg PA
CBHW081309040426
42452CB00014B/2709